Lambs, Lambs, Lambs

Denzel T. Carter

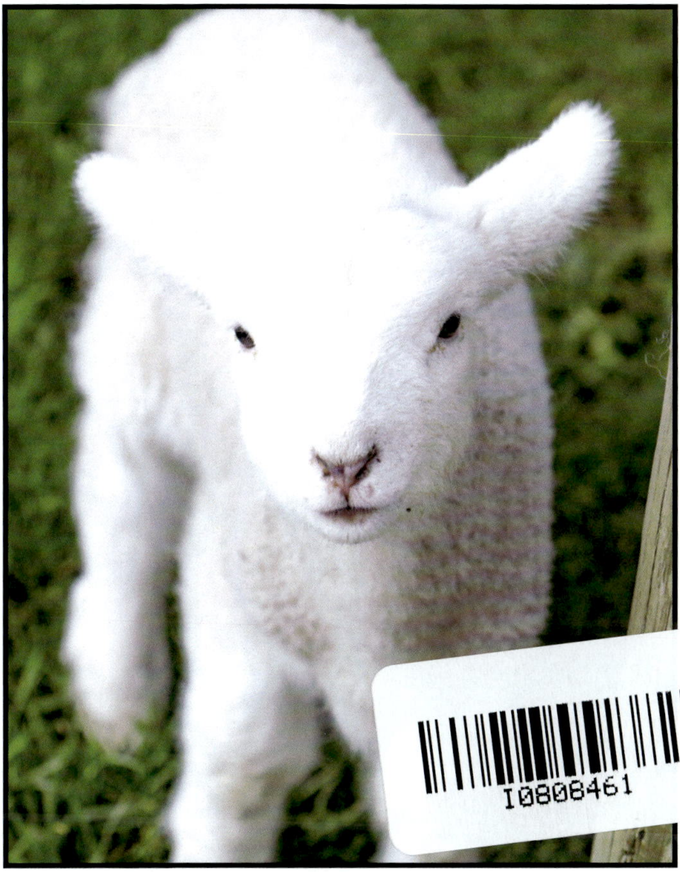

Rosen REAL READERS

Rosen Classroom™
New York

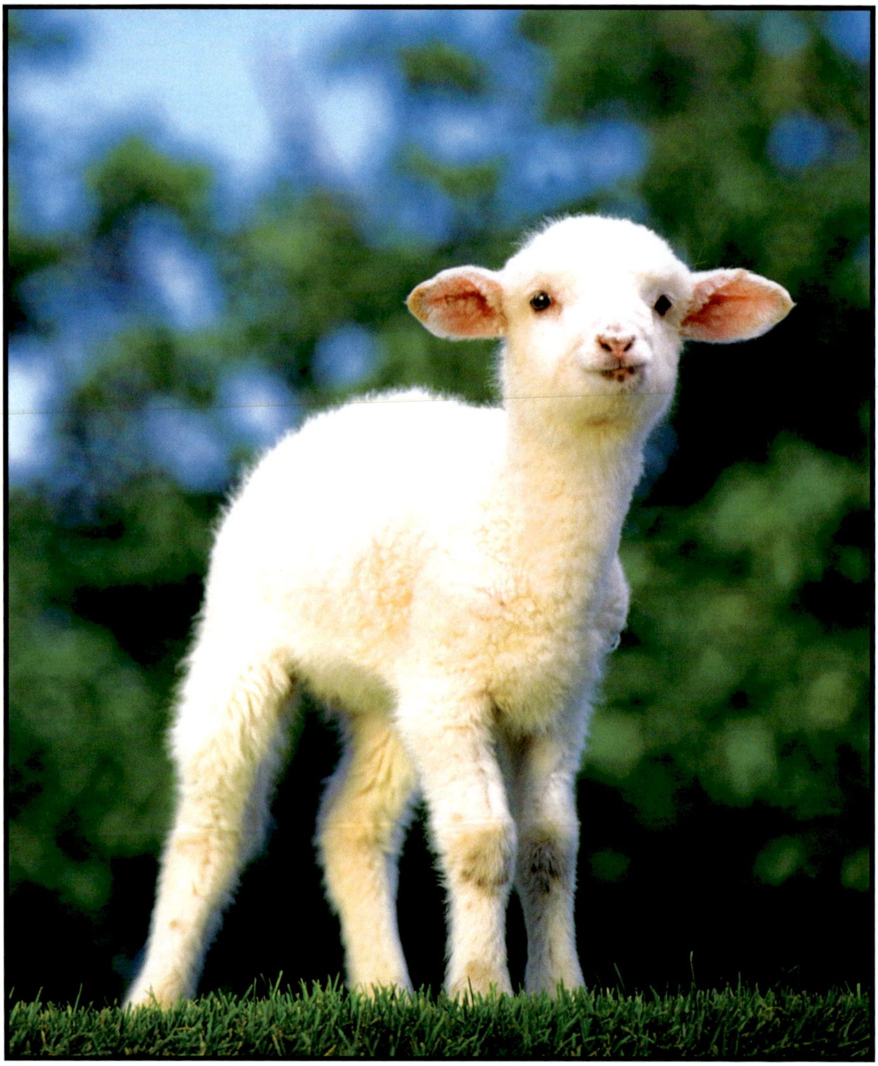

A lamb is a baby sheep.

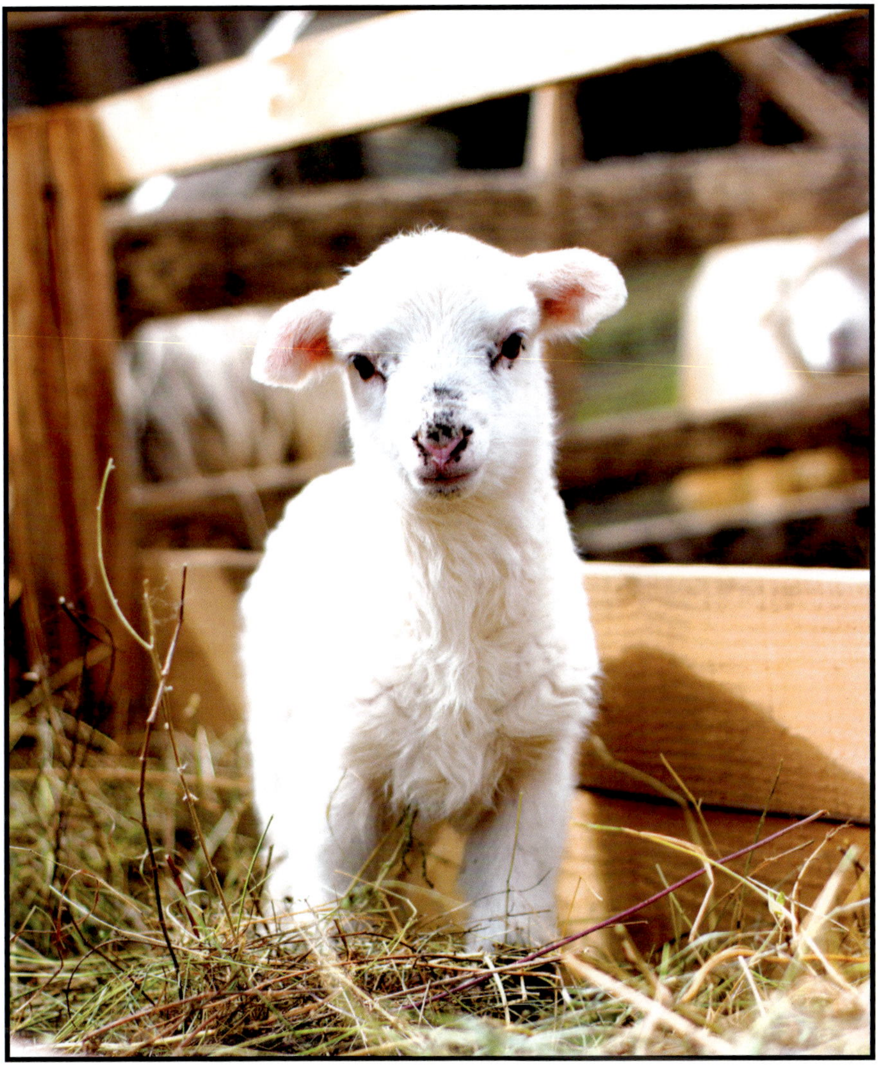

Lambs live on a farm.

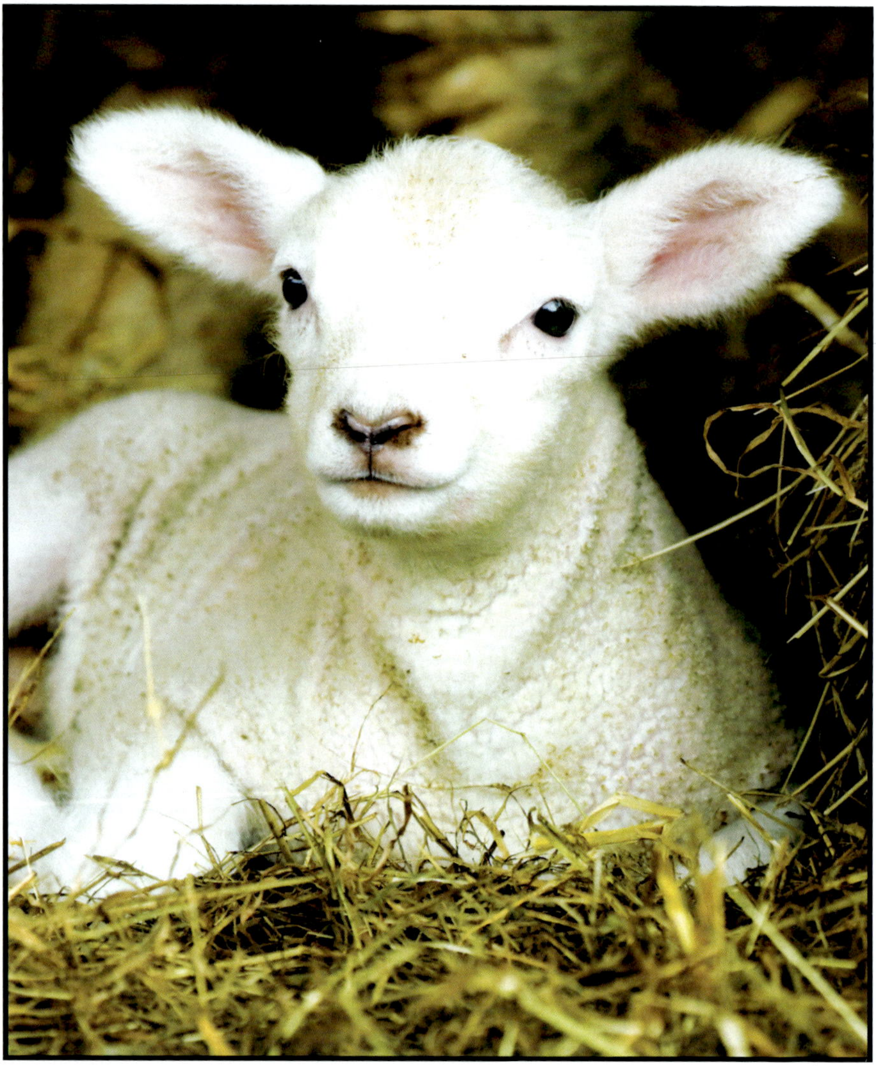

Lambs are white.

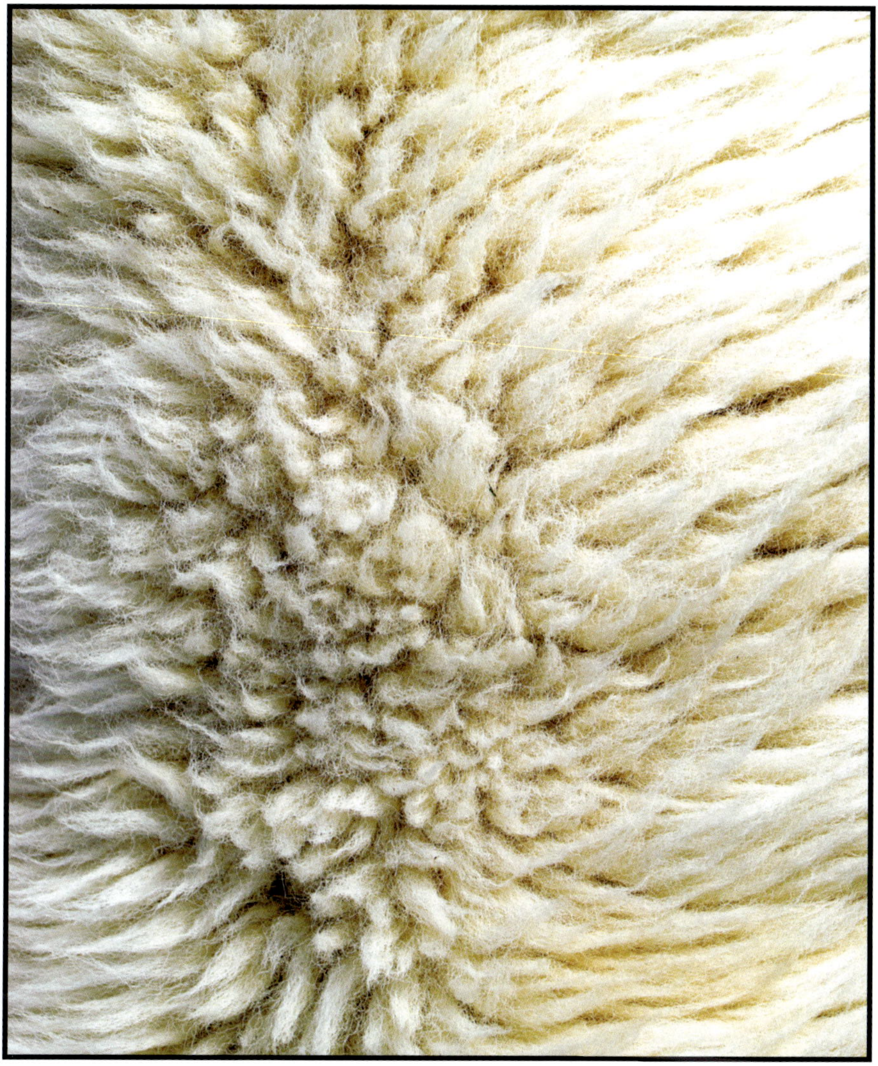

They have fur.

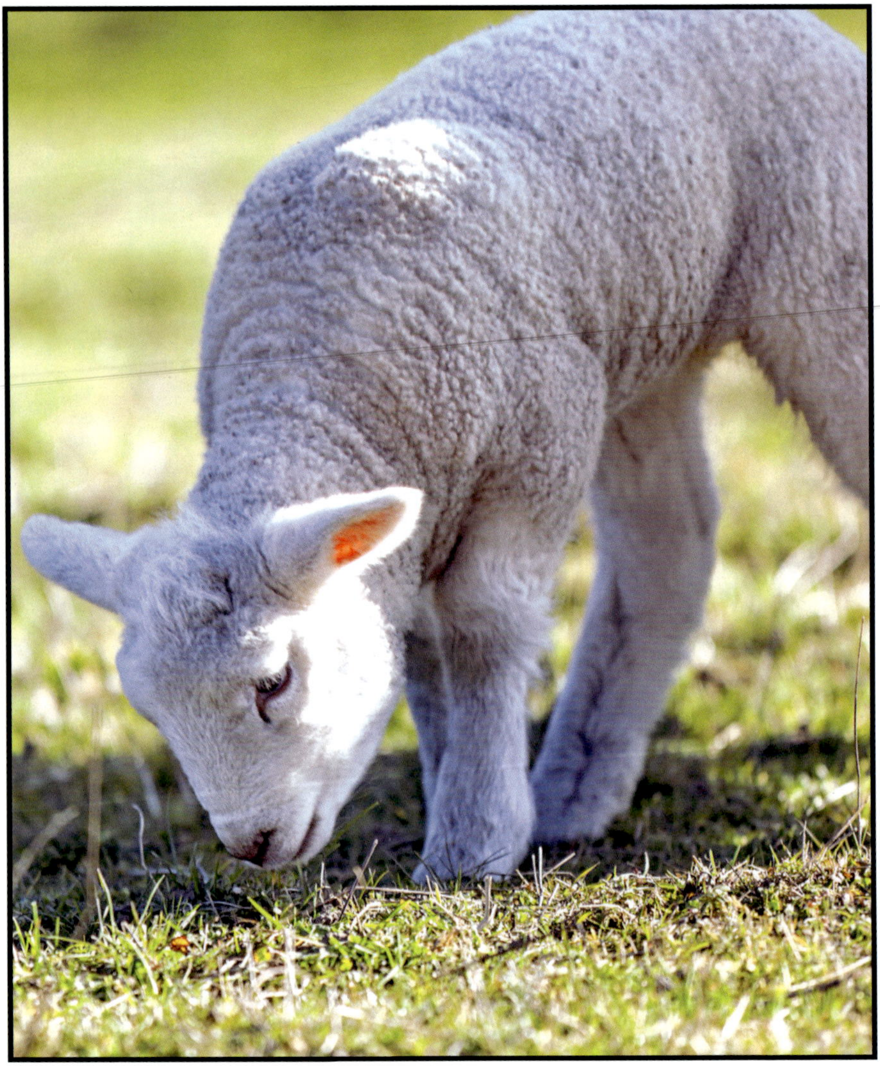

Lambs eat grass.

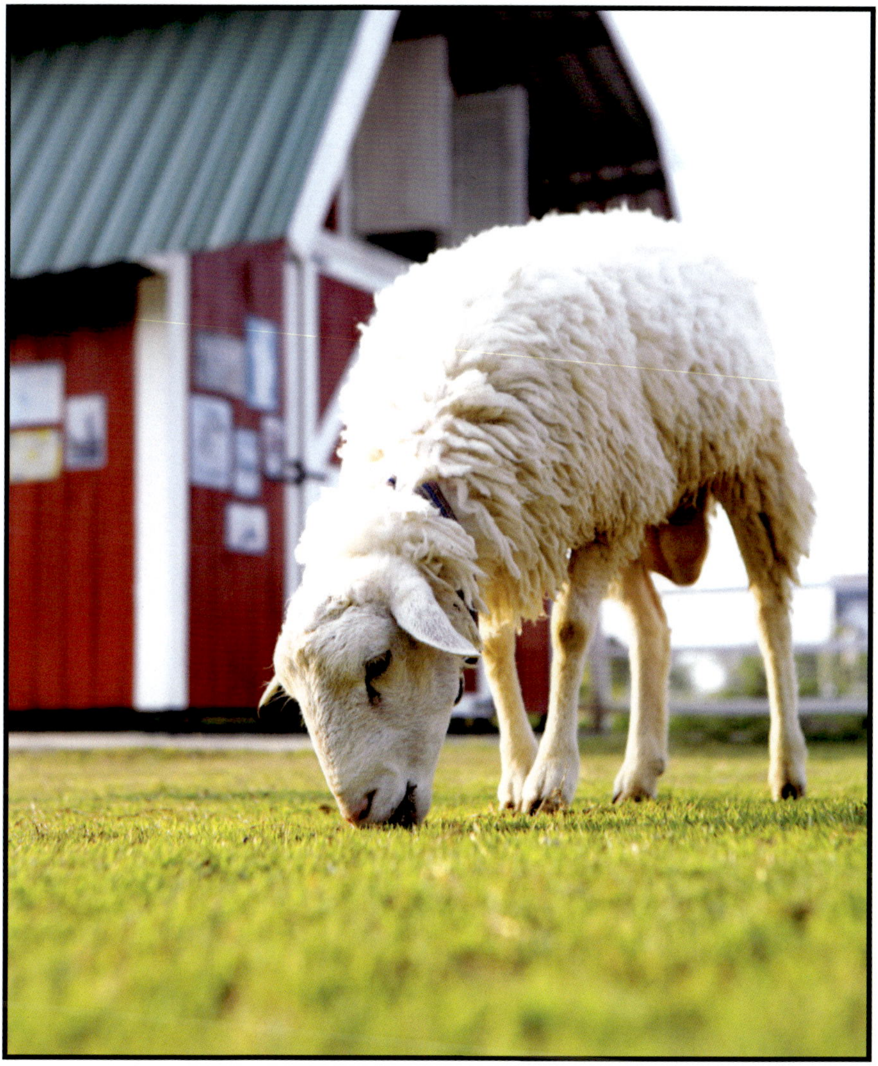

Lambs grow to be sheep.

Words To Know

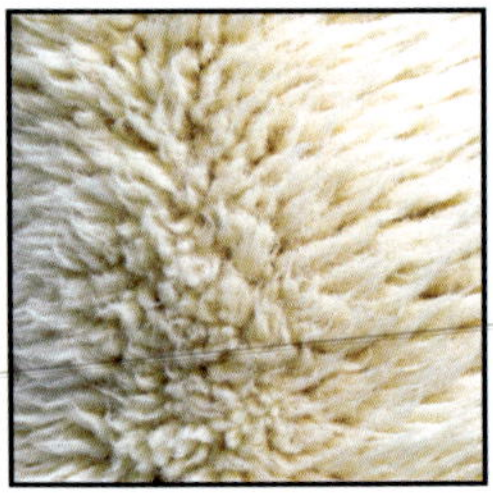

fur

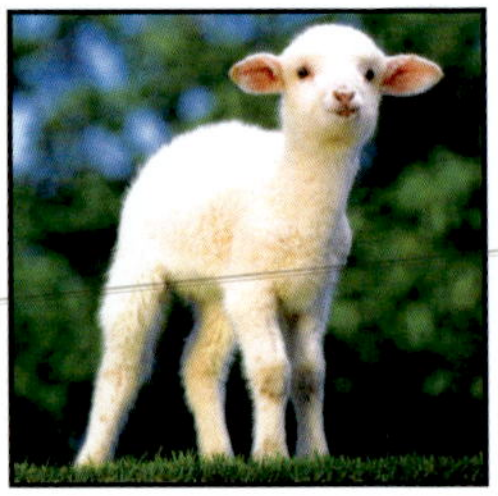

lamb

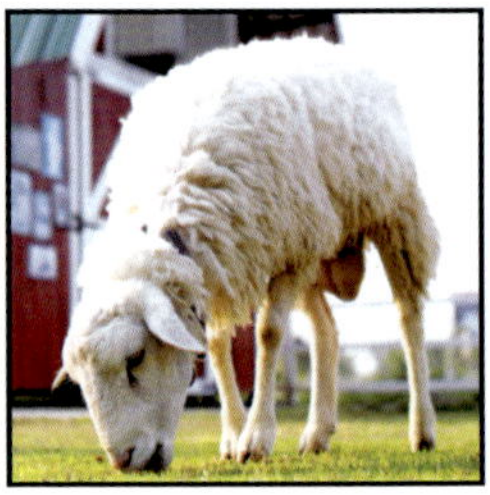

sheep

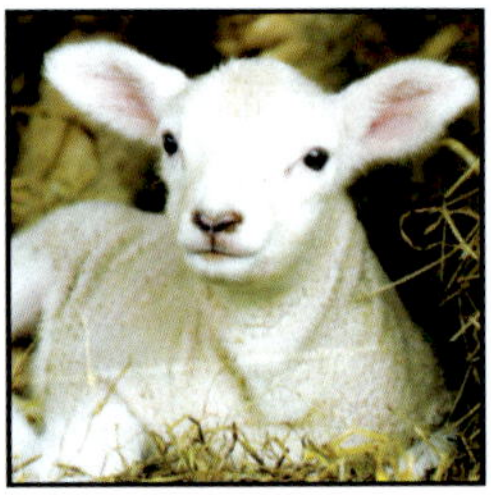

white